A GIFT FOR:

_____

FROM:

_____

DATE:

_____

Crazy About My Cat

BARBOUR
PUBLISHING

ecpa Member of the
Evangelical Christian
Publishers Association

Crazy About My Cat

ALL THINGS BRIGHT AND BEAUTIFUL,
ALL CREATURES GREAT AND SMALL,
ALL THINGS WISE AND WONDERFUL,
THE LORD GOD MADE THEM ALL.
~ Cecil Frances Alexander

I'M CRAZY ABOUT MY CAT BECAUSE
HE GETS ALONG SO NICELY
WITH THE NEIGHBOR'S DOG.

I'M CRAZY ABOUT MY CAT BECAUSE
SHE IS SWEET AND CUDDLY
AND LETS ME RUB HER TUMMY.

I'M CRAZY ABOUT MY CAT BECAUSE
HE ENJOYS SPENDING A LAZY SUNDAY
AFTERNOON THE SAME WAY I DO.

I'M CRAZY ABOUT MY CAT
BECAUSE SHE HAS A SOPHISTICATED
SENSE OF TASTE — SHE
WON'T EAT JUST ANYTHING!

I'M CRAZY ABOUT MY CAT BECAUSE
I KNOW HE UNDERSTANDS WHAT
HE'S WATCHING ON TV.

I'M CRAZY ABOUT MY CAT BECAUSE
SHE DOESN'T HAVE TO SLOBBER
TO TELL ME SHE LOVES ME.

I'M CRAZY ABOUT MY CAT
BECAUSE HE REALLY GETS
INTO THE CHRISTMAS SPIRIT.

I'M CRAZY ABOUT MY CAT BECAUSE
SHE HAS A REAL EAR FOR MUSIC.

I'M CRAZY ABOUT MY CAT BECAUSE
HE'S QUITE THE ACROBAT.

I'M CRAZY ABOUT MY CAT BECAUSE
SHE TURNS TO ME AND HOLDS ON
TIGHT WHEN SHE'S FRIGHTENED.

I'M CRAZY ABOUT MY CAT BECAUSE
HE LOVES FAMILY GAME NIGHT.

I'M CRAZY ABOUT MY CAT BECAUSE
HE IS AN EXCELLENT LISTENER.

I'M CRAZY ABOUT MY CAT BECAUSE
SHE LOOKS SO PRETTY AFTER HER BATH.

I'M CRAZY ABOUT MY CAT BECAUSE
HE HELPS ME DECIDE WHEN IT'S
TIME TO GET NEW FURNITURE.

I'M CRAZY ABOUT MY CAT BECAUSE
I KNOW ALL CATS GO TO HEAVEN.

I'M CRAZY ABOUT MY CAT BECAUSE
HE HAS A BEAUTIFUL SINGING VOICE.

Aren't you just beautiful?!

I'M CRAZY ABOUT MY CAT
BECAUSE SHE HAS A DRAMATIC
SENSE OF FASHION.

I'M CRAZY ABOUT MY CAT BECAUSE
HE IS THOUGHTFUL TO BRING ME
PRESENTS HE'S SURE I'LL LIKE.

I'M CRAZY ABOUT MY CAT BECAUSE SHE
DOESN'T HAVE TO GO OUTSIDE ON
A RAINY NIGHT TO TAKE CARE OF
HER PERSONAL BUSINESS.

I'M CRAZY ABOUT MY CAT
BECAUSE HE CLEANS UP
AFTER HIMSELF.

I'M CRAZY ABOUT MY CAT
BECAUSE SHE IS PERFECTLY
CONTENT TO PLAY BY HERSELF.

I'M CRAZY ABOUT MY CAT BECAUSE
HE WAS BORN SMART AND WITH
GOOD MANNERS — AND HE DIDN'T HAVE
TO ATTEND OBEDIENCE SCHOOL.

I'M CRAZY ABOUT MY CAT BECAUSE
SHE KNOWS HOW TO ATTRACT A CROWD.

I'M CRAZY ABOUT MY CAT
BECAUSE HE'S BETTER THAN
ANY OLD ALARM CLOCK.

I'M CRAZY ABOUT MY CAT BECAUSE
SHE COMES FROM ROYALTY.

I'M CRAZY ABOUT MY CAT
BECAUSE I KNEW THE MOMENT
I SAW HIM HE WAS MINE!

I'M CRAZY ABOUT MY CAT BECAUSE
OF HER RESILIENT SPIRIT.

(SHE HANGS IN THERE EVEN IN THE TOUGH TIMES.)

I'M CRAZY ABOUT MY CAT BECAUSE
HE ABSOLUTELY ADORES OTHER PETS.

I'M CRAZY ABOUT MY CAT BECAUSE
SHE HAS AN INCREDIBLE SENSE
OF SMELL THAT HELPS HER
FIND HER WAY HOME.

I'M CRAZY ABOUT MY CAT BECAUSE
HE KEEPS ME ON MY TOES.

I'M CRAZY ABOUT MY CAT
BECAUSE SHE HAS
AN INCREDIBLE APPRECIATION
FOR MODERN ART.

I'M CRAZY ABOUT MY CAT BECAUSE
HE DOESN'T CHASE CARS!

I'M CRAZY ABOUT MY CAT
BECAUSE SHE REALLY IS A
MEMBER OF THE FAMILY.

I'M CRAZY ABOUT MY CAT BECAUSE
HE KNOWS THERE'S A TIME TO FIGHT —
AND A TIME FOR FLIGHT!

I'M CRAZY ABOUT MY CAT BECAUSE I'M
NOT SURE IT'S EVER REALLY HER FAULT.

I'M CRAZY ABOUT MY CAT BECAUSE
HE ALMOST ALWAYS KEEPS HIS POISE.

I'M CRAZY ABOUT MY CAT BECAUSE
SHE IGNORES PETTY ANNOYANCES.

I'M CRAZY ABOUT MY CAT BECAUSE
HE IS ALWAYS READY TO
CLEAN UP AFTER DINNER.

I'M CRAZY ABOUT MY CAT BECAUSE
SHE UNDERSTANDS MY MOODS.

I'M CRAZY ABOUT MY CAT
BECAUSE HE IS SIMPLY
PUR-R-R-R-FECT FOR ME!

I'M CRAZY ABOUT MY CAT BECAUSE
SHE KNOWS HOW TO AMUSE HERSELF —
EVEN IF I HAVE TO BE GONE
FOR AN ENTIRE DAY.

I'M CRAZY ABOUT MY CAT BECAUSE
HE HAS THE QUIET CONFIDENCE OF
SOMEONE WHO JUST KNOWS
HE IS GOOD LOOKING.

I'M CRAZY ABOUT MY CAT BECAUSE
EVEN WHEN SHE PRETENDS TO BE COOL,
DEEP DOWN I KNOW SHE TRULY LOVES ME.

I'M CRAZY ABOUT MY CAT BECAUSE
HE REMINDS ME TO SLOW DOWN
AND SAVOR GOD'S CREATION.

I'M CRAZY ABOUT MY CAT BECAUSE
SHE UNDERSTANDS THAT GOOD FRIENDS
DO NOT ALWAYS REQUIRE WORDS
WHEN THEY'RE TOGETHER.

I'M CRAZY ABOUT MY CAT BECAUSE HE WAS
CREATED BY A GOD WHO THINKS CATS ARE GREAT!

GOD LOOKED OVER
EVERYTHING
HE HAD MADE;
IT WAS SO GOOD,
SO VERY GOOD!

GENESIS 1:31